Conscious Parenting: A Guide to Living with Young Children

by
Stephen Spitalny

Conscious Parenting:
A Guide to Living with Young Children

©2015 by Stephen Spitalny

First Printing 2015

ISBN 978-1-329-05494-3

Chamakanda Press

www.chamakanda.com

Conscious Parenting: A Guide to Living with Young Children

by
Stephen Spitalny

Contents

Introduction   7

1. Some Aspects of Early Childhood Development   9

2. Imitation   13

3. The Young Child as Total Sense Organ   15

4. The Responsibility for the Satisfaction of the Needs   17
   of Young Children Falls to the Adults Caring for Them

5. I Got Rhythm   19

6. Some Specific Communication Tools and Tips   23
   and a Look at Some Habits of Communication

7. I Want To Be a Responder Not a Reactor,   39
   So How Do I Work On Myself?

8. Conflict Resolving   55

9. Smile and Enjoy   71

10. RSVP   73

Bibliography   75

Introduction

The human being is provided with certain tools including the vast potential of our head and heart. The head functions better when it has some information and understanding. Learning to listen to what your own heart is saying and then having a conversation between your head and heart is what guides you through the challenging times.

The essence of being human is connecting. We need to relate to others, and we automatically try to relate any experience to ones we have already experienced. The given fact of our need to relate and connect with others does not imply we are able to do it well. Most of us have to learn how to truly connect, and we have to undo various habits that are obstacles to connecting.

In this book I want to offer some basic principles to help you through the challenging moments that will arise in your life with young children. This book includes many tools for you to use. If these are taken up, you will experience an enhancement of your connecting with young children and an increase in your awareness of yourself. Taking up the principles and offered practices will also enhance your connecting with anyone.

Some of the ideas and principles in this book are repeated several times. That was consciously done to stress the importance of those basic thoughts. If you notice something being repeated, then know that I think it is important.

Recently I saw a flyer for a class claiming to teach parents how to have "listening and cooperation" in relating to their young children. I read the text on the flyer and realized that this was a class to get young children to do what you tell them. I have a different understanding about listening and cooperation. In this book I want to share with you some ideas about what I think is true listening - to both the words and the underlying needs of your young children.

Now I have a question for YOU.
Why are you reading this book?

We live in a culture of needing experts. We seek out experts for many things because we have been conditioned to think we can't do it ourselves. Our confidence has been eroded.

My intention in writing this book is not to offer a trail map, but to strengthen your own inner compass. My hope is that in the reading of this book, and in the doing the real work of taking up some of the suggested practices, you will discover that you are becoming the expert. Learning how to use your head and heart together is the path that can lead to the confidence of being your own expert. In point of fact, you are the only expert for your unique situation.

Chapter 1

Some Aspects of Early Childhood Development

Let's start with a look at early childhood development, both physical development and the development of the sense of self.

Physical Development

One organ that deserves a special look is the brain, the physical organ where capacities for memory, thinking and creativity are based. This has a direct bearing on our subject at hand as you will soon see.

One way of thinking about the brain is the so-called "triune brain" (as described by Paul MacLean). There are three major functional systems in the brain that each have a specific role. The most ancient part of the brain is called the 'reptilian brain.' It is the 'survival brain' and operates instinctual responses such as fight and flight, aggression and dominance.

The limbic system can be thought of as the emotions and feelings system. It first appeared in the early mammals in the course of evolution. The most recent addition in brain evolution is the neocortex which Maclean described as "the mother of invention and father of abstract thought."

The most advanced part the neocortex system is the prefrontal cortex, also called the frontal lobe. The prefrontal cortex is the part of the brain that plans, reasons and is responsible for impulse control. In the individual, the prefrontal cortex is the last portion of the brain to fully develop, it is not finished and mature until one's late 20's. This means that **young children do not develop complex decision-making and planning skills until much later** in their development. With young children (whose prefrontal cortex is barely developed) adults might be spending a lot of time trying to explain to them, even though their brain is not ready for the type of understanding the adult is expecting.

The prefrontal cortex is responsible for reasoning. The prefrontal cortex is responsible for planning.

I repeat; the part of the brain that is key to reasoning, problem solving, comprehension, and impulse-control is the prefrontal cortex. These executive brain functions are needed when we have to focus and think, mentally play with ideas, use our short-term working memory, and thinking before reacting in any situation. Please do not assume there to be a more developed neurology in the young child than is even possible.

The possibility inherent in the adult who has a more advanced neurology and intellect is to **understand** what the child's needs are, and her level of development - and then to be the gentle yet firm guide she is looking for.

One problem is that when someone's needs are not being met, reaction habits kick in. These habits are the reptile brain trying to make the environment safer for the individual. As we all know, these habits often are not helpful or successful in getting those needs met. We adults need to recognize our own habits and find ways to overcome them by allowing our own prefrontal cortex to lead and choose what we want to do and say.

There are other aspects of physical development worth a quick look. When a baby is born, all of the sense organs are operational. They send signals to the brain. What is not yet operational is the processing capacity to make connections between the sensory perceptions. There is plenty of perception but there is no conceptualizing to connect those perceptions.

During the young child's first couple of years there is a vast development of neural pathways and neural structure to put in place the necessary hardware to process sensory information. Just looking at the baby's body you see how large the head is in proportion to the trunk and limbs. This underscores the fact that major growth and development is happening in the head during the first few years.

Between 2-years and 5-years-old, the trunk has a significant increase in size. What is going on? The thoracic and abdominal organs are having a field day of growth. The lungs, heart, liver, kidneys and all are developing at a faster rate than the rest of the body. They are growing in size and maturing in functioning.

Sometime after five years, the child's limbs significantly lengthen and their overall proportions resemble that of an adult's, only smaller. This is why people say children grow from the head down.

A critical task for the young child is the development of his own physical body. Pushing him into premature intellectual activity is to the detriment of organ development and the healthy growth of the body.

If you only take away one thing from reading this section, this is it: *Young children do not have complex decision-making and planning skills until much later in their development because their prefrontal cortex is immature and relatively undeveloped.*

The Development of the Sense of Self

Another aspect of early childhood development that is essential to understand in guiding us toward conscious relating with young children is the development of the sense of self.

At birth, the baby is awash in new experiences. Every sensory experience is as new. The newborn is truly at one with her world. She does not have an experience of self as separate from the world. She does not experience herself as separate from mom or dad. She does not experience herself as separate from the rug, or the blanket, or the sounds, smells and tastes. The feeling of being a separate self arises slowly and gradually. Some milestones on this trajectory include; standing and walking (often walking away from mom and dad), calling herself "I," realizing at about 9-years-old that her inner world of thoughts is not accessible to parents and others, and teenage years pushing away from parents. All these are parts of the pathway of discovery and the solidification of experiencing a separateness of self.

From the point of view of the development of the sense of self, the newborn is totally asleep. She has no concept of self separate from other. An adult is fully aware of herself as a self, a separate entity from others and the world around her. The experience of separateness is gradually developing in young children so their experience of self is as if in a dream. As they get older, more and more they relate to the world from a self.

An interesting part of this development is the phase often called the "terrible twos." At this stage, the toddler regularly says 'No' to whatever she is told to do (or not do). This can be very challenging for parents. One thing that can help is understanding that when she says 'no' to you, she is saying 'yes' to herself. "No, that is not me. That is not me. No. That is not me. No. I am not that. I am not you." No means yes to self at this stage.

Another way to think of it is that young children live very much in the periphery of their experience, in their surroundings, and as they develop an experience of self, then more and more they relate to the world from their own center.

Young children have an undeveloped awareness of self and are much more connected with what is around them than adults are.

Chapter 2

Imitation

For the young child, imitation is the primary learning modality. So many elements of our human-ness are developed in the early years and they are developed through a process of imitation. Among these learned skills are walking, speaking, and methods for dealing with stress and challenges. Humans only learn to walk and speak by copying other human beings! And we develop our habits of dealing with challenging situations and our communication habits, by copying. These habits are firmly entrenched by age three or earlier.

A key neurological element involved in imitation is mirror neurons These neurons 'fire' both when an child acts and when the child observes an action performed by another. It is the same with any age - mirror neurons are engaged when we receive through our senses information (sights, sounds, etc.) about what someone else is doing. They stimulate 'motor' neurons **as if** we were doing the moving or speaking. Mirror neurons are important for understanding the actions of other people, and for learning new skills by imitation.

With human beings, imitation is of much greater significance than other creatures of the earth. A newborn horse will stand up within the first hour after its birth, can trot and canter within hours, and most can gallop by the next day, even if you remove all other horses from the foal's environment. The foal will also "speak" like a horse without other horses around to imitate.

A human being will never learn to stand, walk or speak like a human unless there are human walkers and speakers to imitate. These three human capacities of walking, speaking and thinking are developed by imitation and are founded on each other.

At first, the baby makes random movements. Repeating and repeating these random movements develops the neural pathways that allow the control of the baby's own movement to gradually arise. By copying the human walkers around her, the baby learns to walk. Speaking becomes possible because fine motor skill is developing to control the various fine muscle activity involved in creating speech sounds, from jaw movement, air, tongue and lips, to the vocal cords in the larynx. The sounds are copied from the human speakers around her. Speaking is a foundation for thinking because most human beings think in words. First we have to develop vocabulary, syntax and grammar, and then we can think.

Let me repeat; When human babies are born, they cannot walk or talk. How they learn to walk and speak is by copying the other human beings in their environment. If they were not around other human beings they would not learn how to walk and speak like a human. (For example the 'wolf child of Aveyron'). The children also learn many other things from parents through imitation, notably their strategies to deal with frustration and stress.

Mirror neurons are active when we are learning to walk and to speak. The child's motor nerves are stimulated when seeing someone else walk, perhaps as preparation for their own walking. The same with the vocal system. When watching and hearing someone speak, the larynx and related organs are stimulated to move in a similar fashion as the speaker's. This continues our whole life.

It is crucial to understand the role of imitation in learning for the young child. When we grasp the implications of this fact, we have to look at ourselves to see if we say and do what we want the children to imitate. **Since the primary learning modality for the young child is imitation, what we do and say, and who we are as adults standing before them is of the utmost importance.**

Chapter 3

The Young Child as Total Sense Organ

Through the senses we receive images, or information, by which we learn to relate to ourselves, the world around us and each other. The senses provide the information by which one is able to be active and engage. The young child experiences the world and herself through sense perceptions.

From the information, or images, received as sense impressions there arise responses or reactions in thoughts, feelings and/or actions. These are the ways with which human beings can interact with the world. We can have an experience which gives us the **perceptions**. We can **think** about an experience, **feelings** can arise, and we can take **action**. Human beings have the capacities for perceiving, thinking, feeling and willing (or taking action). Young children are primarily will-oriented beings. They have an impulse toward actively imitating what they perceive. They are driven to *do* what they *see*. Their thinking is still in a sleeping form as described earlier in the section on physical development.

Also at work in the young child are other levels of sense experience, not perceivable by most adults. Children before age seven directly experience the moods of the adults in their environment, and what adults are feeling and thinking. Most of us have had experiences of having a thought about something, not speaking it out loud, yet a young child says something to us as if hearing our thoughts. The young child is wholly a sense organ, a bit like a sponge, soaking in all levels of experience into the process of forming their physical body and their soul life. So the thoughts and feelings of the adults are perceived (though without understanding) by the young child. All the more reason to develop clarity of thinking, and compassionate attitudes!

Much more so than adults, the nature of young children is to be continuously sensing and doing.

Chapter 4

The Responsibility for the Satisfaction of the Needs of Young Children Falls to the Adults Caring for Them.

One can analyze the basic needs of the human being in various ways. Rick Hanson considers Safety, Satisfaction and Connection as the primary needs. For the young child, adults have to provide the environment that is safe, and adults have to ensure that hunger and thirst and cleanliness needs are satisfied for the child. And adults have to offer real connection, warmth and love. (For more; rickhanson.net)

Another way to think about basic needs is offered by David Richo. He lists the *five A's* -attention, appreciation, affection, acceptance and autonomy - as the primary human needs. Adults have to provide satisfaction of these needs for the baby and the young child because they cannot yet mediate their own needs. (davericho.com)

Additionally, young children cannot understand or articulate their needs. Their feelings and needs live in them in a non-conscious way so it is up to the adults to observe, and then intuit how to meet the child's needs.

Adults also can help the child begin to be able to name their own feelings. For instance, if you observe your child looking downcast, you can say,
"You're sad." "No I'm not. I'm mad."
And now you have helped each other learn something important.

Whatever way you categorize basic needs, children whose basic needs aren't met in early childhood develop into adults who struggle with attempting to get their needs met, often in unhealthy ways, and don't have a feeling of the satisfaction of their needs - it can never be enough.

Our young children surely can't always get what they want, but it is up to their adults to make sure the children get what they need.

Chapter 5

I Got Rhythm

When there is daily rhythm, a regular order of events in the child's day, when her day flows from one thing to the next in much the same way each day, she feels secure in that flow. And there is much less conflict! When I use the term 'rhythm,' I do not mean a rigid schedule or routine, but a flowing in much the same way the tide has a rhythm.

The young child is developing her organs and the relationship of those organs to each other. In the adult each of the organs has a functional rhythm. We can support the developing of the child's organic rhythm by surrounding her with a daily life rhythm - the child's developing organs are immersed in the outer rhythm of life. The young child is in a process of developing her own rhythm of her organs, her relation to the world around them, and the social rhythms of interaction. We can support the child by establishing and maintaining a daily rhythm and there is an amazing side effect. It makes adults' lives less stressful because there is less conflict and argument.

Here are some rhythms to consider:

Sleeping/waking - Is the child getting enough sleep? (Read the book *The 7 0'Clock Bedtime* by Inda Schaenen.) What about an after lunch nap? Are her awake hours active enough so she sleeps well? Are her last few hours before bed each evening free from all electronic media? It physiologically interferes with sleep.

Having an after-dinner routine that carries all the way to sleep time is important. Here is an idea - dinner, then bath and brushing teeth. Then into bed for story and sleep. Every day just like this. After the first few days you won't hear, "I don't want to brush my teeth." It has just become what you do. Every day. You can't argue with it just like the tides. It just happens.

It is up to the adult to establish the rhythm and make sure it is supported.

Does your child wake up on her own in the morning? Or do you have to awaken her to be ready for the day's scheduled events? Make bedtime early enough so that she naturally wakes up in time to eat and dress before you have to take her to day-care or school.

Of course there will be deviations from the rhythm. It is not so rigid. Holiday dinner at grandma's house will deviate from the norm - our rhythm has to be able to flex to include what comes up in life.

Family rhythm functions as a structure from which we can meet life with flexibility.

Eating/Not Eating

Do some of her meltdowns happen because of low blood sugar? Does an extra snack time need to regularly be put into the day? Is there sufficient time of not-eating to allow the digestive system to work? If your child "grazed" all afternoon and then is not hungry at dinner time, something needs to shift.

Perhaps a not-eating time for a few hours before dinner could help. In a family, not everyone's digestive system rhythm is the same. We can find a rhythm that fits most and then maybe for one family member, an extra afternoon snack is needed. It is up to the adults to assess the real food needs of the children, and create the rhythm accordingly.

The best thing you can do for to create a family rhythm is start with a consistent dinner time. Have dinner at the same time each day. This will ripple into the rest of the day because if dinner time is consistent, then after dinner activities leading up to bed time will become consistent. And waking up in the morning will become consistent.....Your life will be easier, your child's life and your child's care provider or teacher's will too.

Hand washing before eating - Make this part of the flow of your day and eventually you won't be nagging your child to wash her hands.

To create a rhythm of your day, think it through. What do you want in the day, and what do the children need. Then, be consistent in establishing and maintaining that rhythm. Watch to see that the needs of the children and other family members are being met. Adjust your rhythm if necessary to better meet the needs. Then relax and enjoy the lower level of stress you have created for your life and your child's. This is one way adults with developed prefrontal cortex can work with the environment to make the lives of all family members flow more smoothly.

Young children live much more in the present moment than we adults do. Their development, as well as their sense of security and well-being, is supported by structure and regularity. Having a daily family life rhythm with regular timing for daily routines supports mental and emotional health and less anxiety for all involved.

Daily rhythm is a blessing for the developing person and for the adults around her. Creating a healthy rhythm is a secret "discipline" for everyone involved.

Remember this formula:

Rhythm = less conflict.

Chapter 6

Some Specific Communication Tools and Tips, and a Look at Some Habits of Communication

Remember that the primary learning method for young children is imitation. **Instructing, explaining, scolding, threatening, bribing and moralizing are not effective methods.** Young children don't learn from these methods, though they can be 'trained' or 'conditioned.' True learning only happens when the initiative for action is coming from inside - then there is a possibility for learning to arise. We only learn when we do it ourselves.

Imitation is the young child's technique for taking hold of the world around her. The impulse for imitation is external - what is sensed by the child all around her (outer). The (inner) will of the child is what takes hold and does the imitating. In the young child this is not a conscious process. She do not choose what she wants to learn through imitating. The possibility of deciding what you want to learn and then attempting to learn it comes much later in life.

Based on physical/neurological development, and the development of the sense of self in the young child, here is a list of some suggestions of what I consider to be some **Effective Communication Practices:**

1. **Speak Less.** Adults speak so much, more than young children have a possibility of paying attention to. If you have something that must be said to your child, then before you speak, condense it into just a few words. Consider, "Can I get this across in less than a dozen words?" Think before you speak and say what you need to say concisely.

Before you nag, remind, criticize, advise, chime in, or over-explain, say to yourself; **'W.A.I.T' (Why am I talking?)** Try to listen more than you talk.

This first practice is using the acronym W.A.I.T. as a mantra. I stumbled this acronym and I wish I could claim credit as the author. It is incredibly useful.

Think first, then talk. W.A.I.T. - Why am I talking? Take this mantra as a moment of pause when your reaction pattern tries to kick in, when your button has been pressed. Say it over and over and over. What **am I** thinking? **WAIT.** What do I want to say? Do I need to say anything? What if I take one breath, or two, or three, before saying or doing anything? Can I shorten whatever I think needs to be said into it's essential few words to get across to my young child what I really want? Do I even need to intervene in this at all? Why aren't I thinking? **W.A.I.T.**

2. **Speak Slowly.** Young children cannot process words as fast as adults. To have your words understood, slow them down. When adults do speak to children, it is sensible to be aware of the speed of our speaking. Adults tend to talk fast, especially when the subject seems important to the adult. Yet actively slowing down our speaking can often be all it takes for our message to get through.

One research project looked at the rate of adults' speech in relation to the processing capacity of the developing central nervous system in young children. The researchers found that in general adults speak too rapidly and can overload children's central nervous systems which inhibits the child's ability to learn. The study showed that the average adult speaks between 160 and 170 words per minute (wpm) while the average child age five to seven years old can process speech at a maximum rate of 124 wpm. When teachers and parents speak more quickly than young children can process, the intended message cannot get across. In the young child, what may sometimes appear as inattention is simply not being able to process at the speed with which the words were spoken.

Slow your speaking down.

If you slow down your rate of speech the sounds become more distinct, the vowels and consonants sound more clearly for the listening young child. When we begin to speak more slowly we are increasing the possibility of the young child understanding what is being said. (Dinkel, Dana; *WSU professor researches how to speak to children,* Wichita State Univ.)

Once, on the first day of kindergarten a child said to me, "Steve, you talk slow." At our first parent conference a couple of months later, his father asked, "How come he listens to you?"

3. **Speak the Truth.**

Make sure that yes means yes and no means no.

Do you know why children whine? Often it is because they have discovered that when a parent says 'no' to them, whining is an effective technique to turn a 'no' into a 'yes.' If you mean 'no,' be consistent and hold on to your 'no.' If you change your mind, acknowledge it. "I've been thinking and have changed my mind. We are going for ice cream anyway." If you often change from no to yes after the whining starts, then you are affirming and encouraging whining as a method to get what is wanted.

Consistency in follow through.

If you announce to your child that something will or will not happen at some appointed time interval, make sure that it is what happens. Teach by your example that you keep your word about things.

Teaching by example, thereby capitalizing on your young child's impulse for imitation, is far more effective than any instructing or explaining can ever be.

4. Use Your "But" Sparingly!

The word 'but' negates everything before it in the sentence.

"You did put away the toys on the couch *but* there are still toys on the floor to put away."
"I know you want to stay up *but* it's bedtime."

Alternatively you could say:

"You put away the toys on the couch already. Let's put the ones on the floor away too."
"I know you want to stay up and now it is bedtime."

And is a much softer word and does not negate. *And* adds on.

A couple of other words I try to never use and to always leave out are **Never** and **Always**. Most of the time they are not true and they set you up to be inconsistent and not truthful.

5. *No* Is Not a Bad Word. Try Not To Overuse It.

No is not a 'bad' word yet many adults shy away from using it with young children. 'No' is shorthand for "This is a boundary." For some adults it is hard to say 'No' to their young children? Here are some reasons why I think it is so hard.

1. We want our children to be happy and to do and have what they want. We want them to have everything to their hearts' content. We see their sadness when they don't get to do or have what they want. We don't want to say 'No' because it leads to our child's unhappiness.

2. We want our child to like us. If we say 'No' to their desires then they probably won't like us. If we always give them what they want then they *will* like us.

3. We don't want to be thought of as the 'mean' parent. Our child will tell other children, their grandparents and their teachers that we are mean because we don't let them do what they want.

4. We learned of a parenting philosophy in which a parent should never say 'No' to their children because the children will grow up with repressed desires and resentment.

5. All the other parents are saying 'Yes' and you want your child to 'fit in.' And we don't want our children to have to wait for something we will probably eventually give them or let them do anyway. Why not let it be now?

Young children look to us to guide them into life as a human being. Part of that guidance is the delivery of our values for physical and emotional safety, and healthy life habits as expressed by the boundaries and limits we hold for our children. We don't have to explain our values. Explaining is not effective with young children anyway. However, we do have to be clear and consistent with our boundaries for the sake of the child's healthy development, and we can express these boundaries simply and with few words. *"No throwing sand. I want everyone to be safe."* Boundaries are a way for the child to experience our care and values, and leads to the child's feeling of security in the embrace of our care. Even though the child may experience feelings of sadness or anger when they meet our boundaries, the boundaries help to define the child's world and hence they are free to explore within those boundaries. If your boundaries for the children are clear, their life is less anxious because they are not constantly pushing the limits to find the boundaries.

Children are natural explorers and some children experience 'No' much too often in the course of their daily explorations. Their natural impulse to touch and taste and move and drop and experiment is squashed. That surely is not healthy for the child. One approach is to create your young child's home environment so that your prized possessions are not accessible and you won't have to say 'No' so often. Lock up the hazardous stuff, make it inaccessible. Put away the fragile and 'special' things until your child is older and can understand what you want her to touch and what not to, and how to be gentle with certain things. Find ways to create the boundaries without having to use the 'No' word so often. Rather than saying what you don't want, tell your child what you do want. Tell them what they can do. And if you have to say no, also offer what he can do instead. *"No drawing on the wall. You can draw on paper."*

No to this, and yes to that.

As your child gets older, it is important that the boundaries loosen gradually. Boundaries are not static, they need to expand as the child matures and can take more and more self-responsibility. Healthy boundaries for young children lead to taking self-responsibility as they mature.

Advertisers rely on adults to succumb to children's whining. They target children with their ads and packaging. If you must bring your child when you go shopping, it can be a helpful practice to develop the habit of you being one who decides on the purchases, with your child as advisor, not the other way around.

Remember that just because you said, 'No,' once, or even many times, doesn't mean your child won't ask again, or attempt to do the same behavior you already said 'No' to. If we understand that the child is not being malicious and not trying to get us upset (they are not!), then perhaps we can be calmer in our saying 'No' for the hundredth time. Or thousandth.

The child is simply trying to do what he wants and uses the strategies he has already found to be successful from his previous experiences. These strategies were developed through a dynamic interaction with his parents. With us. It is not useful to blame him for not listening, or be angry with him for his purposeful attempt to get us angry. That is not the case. Calmly and patiently we CAN help our children develop new strategies to get what they want, strategies that don't upset those around them. It takes time and repetition - lots of both.

Here are some reasons why experiencing 'No' is important in the life of the young child.

1. Whining is the result of parents not wanting their child to be sad. If a 'No' turns into a 'Yes' in the face of our child's sadness or whining, then our child learns that whining is a very successful strategy to get what she wants. If we allow our child her sadness, then she will develop the capacity to deal with their own sadness. Sadness is one of the basic feelings that undoubtedly will arise at various times in our child's life. Allow children to have their whole range of feelings. I am not saying to purposely orchestrate situations to make your child sad, but learn how to allow the child to have their feelings without you trying to prevent or 'fix' it.

2. Our child will love us all the more for the healthy boundaries and limits we create for her. In the moment she may feel the sadness or anger of desires thwarted, but in the big picture she will feel secure in our care and guidance for her.

> When she was in my kindergarten, Brandi was a 'fireball.' She was lightweight and solid, and she moved easily and smoothly. She was very articulate and intelligent. She tended to be one of the last children to arrive each day, and I noticed from the start that Brandi did not have an easy time joining into the play of the other children. A regular occurrence was her arriving to many other children already engaged in play, houses built and imaginations unleashed in various activities. Brandi would look around the room and then walk toward some play activity and so often what happened next was a house knocked over and another child sad. "Steve, Brandi wrecked our house." I saw that my work was cut out for me because Brandi was very determined to do things her way and if she thought I was trying to

intervene she grew angry. She often shouted, "I can do what I want!"

One morning, Brandi was headed for an elaborate house made out of heavy wooden 'play stands' that looked a bit tentative in terms of stability. Another child was laying on the floor just inside the 'house.' I thought I needed to be close by to make sure everyone was safe and I watched Brandi's arms prepare to push over the side of the house. I learned already that explaining to Brandi would not work, so I walked in between Brandi and the house. I said, "We will leave the house in peace." She tried to get around me and push the wall over. As calmly and gently as possible, I scooped her up and carried her over to the lunch table and sat down.

She seemed quite angry with me by then and said she was "going back over to knock their wall down." So I sat her on my lap and held her, firmly but not tightly. I wasn't angry or triggered. I didn't squeeze her. I didn't raise my voice - in fact I didn't say anything. She squirmed and kicked and told me, "I am going to tell my mom, and she is going to call the police, and they are going to take you away....Let me go so I can knock over their house." I said to her, only once, "I will not let you knock down their house."

She was fired up and her muscles were tense for a minute or two, and I kept her in my firm hold. It was a protective use of force - not to hurt, but to keep everyone safe. To me, safety is a primary need for all, and a primary responsibility of all teachers! I wanted the other children to be safe, and I wanted to help Brandi develop other strategies for joining in with the other children. I didn't want to exclude her from being with us as in a 'time-out.' To me that seems like punishment. I understood that Brandi was simply using a strategy she had developed to get her needs met, a strategy probably developed by the time she was one-year-old. Strategies become habits when they are successful. So Brandi had found a method that worked in her world to get her needs met. The thing is, that strategy didn't feel good to the other people involved.

So my first step in that interaction was to create a boundary, and I represented that boundary. Boundaries are hard to accept. No one likes boundaries. They are what prevent us from getting what we think we want when we want it. They also are where we find out who we are. What we do when we meet a boundary, how we handle the stress and the dissatisfaction tell us something about ourselves.

3. Saying 'No' does not make someone mean. Meanness is when someone intends to make someone else feel bad. Creating boundaries for your child is healthy and important. As long as you have reasons for what you are doing that support your child's development and support the needs of your child and the group, and you have calmness in how you are delivering the boundaries then what other adults think about you is their problem. If they ever ask why we said 'No' we can explain our reasons and then they can think whatever they choose to think.

4. We set limits for our young children so they will feel secure and confident. Without clear boundaries the children might be doing behaviors increasingly outlandish as a way to find the boundaries they unconsciously know they need.

5. We live in a consumer culture where we are trained to say 'Yes' to all sorts of products and services, and get it immediately or sooner. I think experiences of delaying gratification are important so the children can develop capacities for waiting. Honestly, I think our culture is dysfunctional and is causing massive social, economic, health and environmental problems. Going the opposite way from the 'mainstream' usually seems like a really good idea.

When possible, **say what you want instead of what you don't want**. Sometimes saying 'No' is our only option. When Jack is about to step onto the street and we are a few feet behind we say, "No." When Jack is about to get up from the table before everyone is finished, "I want you to sit with us until we all get up." It has a much different quality than, "Don't get up until we are all done."

Sometimes, especially with 2 and 3 year-olds, when they hear 'don't' it can impel them to 'do' just what you said not to. Perhaps they didn't have the intention of doing the thing until they heard you say not to.

Boundaries create a feeling of safety and protection for a child, and nurture the development of self reliance.

Physical and social boundaries are important on the path of a healthy developing sense of self. The self can only find itself when it meets boundaries. It is a boundary when the child has a drive to stand and cannot yet. He experiences the frustration of being unable, and also what it feels like to push through, to keep trying, and develop a new skill or capacity. This is one type of boundary experience. When he runs toward the curb with no sign of slowing before leaping into the street, and the parent loudly says, "Stop!" That is a boundary. He experiences the concern and love coming from the parent, and his trust in his parent grows, even if his words are complaining. It is the same with social boundaries. (Stephen Spitalny, *Connecting With Young Children: Educating the Will*, p.75)

We adults must provide boundaries of physical and social safety for the children. That is how the children experience our values, without intellectual explanation, simply by the child meeting the boundary where play behavior might switch to an unsafe situation or hurting someone else.

Remember that a child cannot understand in the same way as adult - the neurology of the young child is not fully developed.

Children are more likely to respond to our requests when they feel our love and our interest in them. They know when we are seeing their potential, seeing what they are becoming.

For the young child, too much choice leads to insecurity and lack of self reliance. A child expects guidance from adults. Without this guidance, the child is insecure and confused. This insecurity is weakening for the formation of the child's mind and body.

6. What About Praise?

Depending what you read, and when it was written, praise is either helpful for developing self esteem, or hinders the development of self esteem and self confidence. For a time there was a pop-psychology fad saying that praising a child leads to high self esteem. Recent psychological research studies have found that praising and complimenting young children leads to lower self esteem.

In over-praising children, we're doing more harm than good. If you often tell your child she is doing a great job, then she internalizes that she no longer needs to push herself. Confidence only comes from practice, from doing, from trying and failing and trying again.

Regular complimenting of a young child can also create the start of self-judging and is the basis for later self-judgment and self-esteem issues. Much praise is 'social comparison praise.' Even if the praiser is not speaking the comparisons, it starts the inner activity in the child hearing the praise of comparing herself to others. And it takes her out of the moment. Young children best belong fully in the moment, engaged completely with their activity, their exploration of the world. Praise begins the awakening of self-consciousness - different from the natural awakening of a sense of self - a self-consciousness that observes one's own activity and compares it to others.

Specific acknowledging of a child's actions can be an enhancement to connection. Acknowledge the process, don't praise the product. Being specific in acknowledging an action avoids general 'praise.' When you acknowledge how something specific someone else did effects you, you are letting them in on your truth. It is not a value judgement or opinion, it is your authentic truth.

"I like how you brought the bandaids when Sally fell down. It helped me and her."

"I liked that you tasted the broccoli."

"I like that you sat at the table until we all were done."

"I like how the toys were put away so neatly."

Chapter 8 on *Conflict Resolving* takes a look at the specifics of speaking your truth when it is about something you *don't* like.

7. Get Up Out of Your Chair and Don't Shout Across the House

Do you like it when someone shouts across the room for you to do something? If you want your child to come to you and ask something of you rather than shout across the house, then you have to get up out of your chair and go over to them. (Remember that imitation is a powerful learning tool).

Additionally, sometimes there is a way to use your body and your gestures and not even speak to get across your point. A simple index finger to your lips fully conveys the message that you want her to be less loud. Perhaps your boisterous child charges into the kitchen, slamming the door behind. You could calmly go to the door, open it, and then gently close it. Without saying a thing. A gentle hand to the shoulder can convey many things depending on the context, and no words are necessary. Real connecting doesn't always require words.

8. Answer **Children's Questions** with living, moving, imaginative answers.

The young child's later life of thinking is founded on the freedom of movement of body and the movement of her imagination. Rich, active imaginative language of the adult in the child's early years, not abstraction and concrete facts, is what supports the child's developing imagination.

A young child cannot understand in the same way as adult - the neurology is not fully developed, particularly the **frontal lobe**. If you can find a way to answer her questions in a truthful yet also imaginative way, you are serving her developing neurology in the best way. Can we give answers that engage the child in activity, rather than closing her off with fixed concepts or abstract concepts? Can we learn to give answers that are like nourishing food rather than stones to digest?

"Why is it raining?"
"The clouds are full and the plants are thirsty."

Adults tend toward probing and asking (way too many) questions of child. We forget that the memory of the young child functions differently than ours. Her world is very much of the present. Events that have passed are no longer in their consciousness.

9. **The Sounds of Silence**

How often do the children have an opportunity for quiet, or silence? Do we always have to have a background noise? One's inner music and dialog is squashed by constant outer noises. Sometimes we adults don't even notice noise in the environment because we have the faculty to filter it out. Young children do not have those same filters.

Did you ever notice the sound of the fluorescent lights at Costco? If you are able to focus on it you realize it is quite loud.

Do you still notice how many stores and restaurants have music playing or even TV screens on? Maybe we have a cultural fear of silence. It is scary to be left alone with your friends and family and own inner life. Consider leaving your child at home, if at all possible, when you go shopping.

Recent research shows that children, in fact all of us, need time with no stimulation (i.e. no electronic devices) for our creativity to flourish. Boredom creates the medium for creativity to arise.

10. Teaching Manners

If you want your child to be polite, you have to model politeness for her. Of course, manners and politeness are not universally consistent. What would be considered 'good' manners somewhere would be considered rude and discourteous somewhere else. So you have to choose the manners that you are aiming to transfer to your child. And then use those manners. In interactions with your child, in interactions with your partner, in interactions with the cashier at the grocery store, everywhere, model the use of the manners you want your child to exercise.

You don't need to bring it to your child's attention - you simply do it. You don't need to say,"Honey, did you notice how I said 'thank you' at the coffee shop? I'd like you to say 'thank you' too when someone hands you something." In all your interactions, use kindness, courtesy and politeness and your child will likely follow suit.

Additionally, you can magnify the possibilities of imitation by speaking polite words on behalf of your child. For instance, four-year-old Tommy says, "Give me more raisins." So, while handing him some more raisins, you say, "Please can I have more raisins?"

That way you are planting a seed for his own will to take up in imitating your example. You are speaking the words you would be happy if he used. In contrast, when Tommy says, "Give me more raisins," you could say, "Tommy! Say 'Please' and then I'll give you the raisins." Tommy won't actually learn anything from this method. He will do as he is told because he wants to be 'rewarded' with the raisins. By being told what to say Tommy won't be learning manners because he won't be developing those manners out of his own actions.

Similarly, if we notice our 5-year-old daughter knock over another child. One response could be, "Sally! Say you're sorry." And she probably will because we are demanding it. If instead the adult says, "Susie is hurt. Is there anything we can do for her?" then Sally is free to take action out of herself. Her own will can engage and she can offer help and comfort to the injured child in her own way.

So instead of ordering your child to use manners, instead of demanding they say certain words, I suggest considering how best to utilize the learning mechanism of imitation to achieve your goals for manners and kindness. We adults can create situations where the will of the young child can take hold of the wonderful examples we offer through how we say and do things. Try it and see what happens. It works, it really works!

Chapter 7

I Want To Be a Responder Not a Reactor, So How Do I Work On Myself?

Self education is a moral question;
Have I a right to educate the child unless I educate myself?
Margret Meyerkort

Longtime kindergarten teacher and early childhood mentor Margret Meyerkort said again and again something that resounds in my head as a sort of watchword of my personal striving. "Unless I develop myself, what right do I have to stand before the children?"

The basic learning modality of the young child is imitation. Young children imitate what we adults say, what we do, and even more, how we are and who we are in the world. I am a teacher of young children, a parent, a grandparent and a human being. I want to be worthy of 'standing in front of the children.' I want to be worthy of their imitation as much as I can.

Sometimes we hear inner voices of unworthiness and self-doubt, the voices of fears and inadequacy. We don't want to see how imperfect we are. Fears can keep us from truly looking at ourselves. We all have shortcomings and don't live up to our own standards, and we all need the courage to take an honest look at ourselves. I need courage to look at myself especially if I might (and will) find inadequacies and shortcomings. How can I change myself for the better if I don't look to see what needs to be changed?

When I find the things in me that I want to change it can be overwhelming. I do not like what I find, and there is so much to change. I can only keep up my search to know myself if I can find the enthusiasm to keep at it. I need to be passionately persistent in my inner search for self knowledge to be able to carry on with more and more and deeper and deeper discoveries of what I need to change. And I need this fire, this enthusiasm, this passion to make the changes. I need a wellspring of inner strength. Waking up is not easy. Making the changes is not easy.

I truly do want to develop myself to become a free human being. What I mean is that I want to be able to be free to respond in the moment, not to react based on my own lifelong patterns and conditioning. Becoming free requires diligent and persistent work, the hard work of truly waking up.

What do your 'triggers' look like? What happens in you when you get to the 'end of you rope?' What do you do when your 'buttons' are pressed? How do you manage stress?

What happened the last time you lost your temper? Can you think of a time you felt attacked? What did you do? Can you think of a time you thought someone else knew what they should do, it was obvious to you, and they failed to fulfill your expectation? What did you do? How did it feel?

We all have habitual reaction patterns that kick in when we are triggered. Some people name 'the double' or 'the shadow' that which 'takes over' and is the one doing the speaking and doing when those habitual patterns take over. Whatever words you use, they describe the situation when you are not truly conscious and old habits are 'operating you' and determining what you say and do.

Where do these patterns come from? These patterns are strategies we developed as young children in response to the stress of not getting what we wanted when we wanted it. And these patterns are imbedded in us as early as our first year. They come from the example of our immediate family, mostly mom and dad. For the young child, all learning is through imitation, and we parents are giving the children plenty to imitate. They copy how we move, how we walk. They learn to speak by copying our speech. They learn how to deal with stress by copying our reaction patterns, what we do when we are 'triggered.' They learn behaviors from us that we are happy for them to imitate, and they learn the things we do in their presence that we wish we did not offer up for their imitation.

What if when I reach the end of my rope with young children, I could remember how imitation functions and then ask myself, "How do I want to teach my child to respond in this type of situation." Being aware of and awake to my responsibility to the human development of my child can help me reign in my reaction patterns.

As the saying goes, 'we must be the change we want to see.' To do that we must be aware of our actions and words and undo the old patterns we have been using our whole lives.

Did you ever see your child drop something, and then hear her say, "Sh#@t!" ?

When something like that happens, we have options. We can get angry, and scold, and explain why they shouldn't use that word and on and on. Or we can understand that our child heard someone use that word, perhaps when a bag of groceries was dropped, and quite possibly it was us they heard. The child is simply imitating. Remember, imitation is how they learn.

An important part of changing a habit is being aware of the habit in the first place. A useful tool for developing self-awareness is a seemingly simple exercise described by Rudolf Steiner in the early 1900's. It involves looking back over the day. You practice this each night before going to sleep. One way to practice is to sit in a chair (lying down may quickly bring on sleep) and close your eyes. Picture to yourself an image of you sitting in the chair. And then for the next five minutes, go backwards through your day, starting with the moment just before sitting in the chair, and going backwards through the day until first awakening that morning. Steiner suggested that one could do this in about five minutes. It is a quick review, just a brief glance at the various events of the day.

This exercise provides an opportunity to observe yourself, and discover your 'trigger points.' In going backwards, you might notice a moment when you are all worked up about something, and slowly go back a bit until you notice the moment when your 'button was pushed.' What is it exactly that pushed the button? Try to observe without judging yourself and beating yourself up.

In your review, when you find a moment in the day when you had lost your patience, had become reactive, take a few extra seconds. Look closely at the events just before you 'lost it' so you can observe what set you off. Harshly judging yourself is not helpful. Look at the events as a story, and know that you can rewrite the story. The important thing is to notice, simply notice what was the 'trigger' for you. And then continue with your review of the rest of your day.

Remember it is called a *practice*. When we practice something we realize we are trying to improve at it, we are not already perfect at it. This is NOT an exercise in self-judgment. It is a way to discover your own patterns of reaction. Perhaps after observing the same pattern time and again in the nightly review, you might have a spark of awareness in the midst of a situation when you are about to react habitually. "Oh, here I am in a situation where I usually get triggered. How do I want to respond this time?" It might be fleeting, but eventually lasting awareness of your soul habit is created and therefore an opportunity for changing those habits arises. First you see your habits, then you have the possibility of changing them.

Look again and again at yourself with honesty in this daily practice. Try to find your trigger points, to know yourself better and better, and see the patterns of reacting, your personal 'buttons.' This exercise also can allow us to develop compassion and kindness for our own shortcomings.

Can I feel tenderness and compassion for myself in the very faults and weaknesses that I am struggling with?

An additional element of this practice can be added. When you find one of those triggered moments in your review of your day, you could imagine what you could have done differently. How do you wish you had responded? What could you have said or done to change the interaction? If you strongly picture these alternative responses, over and over, you are reprogramming yourself and eventually you will take up a different response in the actual situations that once triggered you.

This is a daily practice - you have to practice it each day for it to be effective. At the end of each day, when you are feeling peaceful and are not distracted, take a few minutes to do this backwards review as an objective observer.

If you can do this every evening before bed you will begin to see your reaction pattern and your 'button.' *Eventually* this practice will result in your sudden awareness in the moment that you are in one of those situations where your 'button' is being pushed but it isn't causing the reaction pattern to set in and you can choose your next words or action. In that moment you have broken out of your conditioned reaction pattern. It might not last, but you have experienced that it is possible. So you continue the daily evening practice and take some steps forward along with your relapses.

Our attempting to better ourselves has significant impact on our child who is imitating all aspects of life around her. The activity of the adult trying to develop new capacities penetrates deeply into the developing child and can bear fruit much later in life.

I want to develop further in myself less reactiveness and more responsiveness, and am actively engaged on this path. Indeed it is a path of development for the human being who is striving toward consciousness.

A nagging voice of self doubt arises saying that it is just not possible. *How can you change they way you are, they way you have always been?* That is the voice of conditioning, the voice from our culture of shame that says you are simply not good enough. (Read *Daring Greatly* by Brene Brown, Ph.D.)

We can overcome this voice by learning how to let go. We do not have to be stuck in the habits and shortcomings that are revealed when we seek to know our self. Working on your self to make changes AND allowing your self to see the changes you create in yourself is an act of creative and mindful thinking. Unwind the old tapes and think for yourself in each moment - true thinking - digesting, contemplating, considering what comes to you, and integrating it with what has gone before, synthesizing, allowing your self-image to move and change and be alive in you is part of the self-discovery and transformation process.

Mindfulness Practice

There are many practices for developing mindfulness. For me, a big support toward more mindfulness is a practice Rudolf Steiner called the 'Six Essential Exercises,' or the **Six Basic Exercises**. Taking up these exercises offers the possibility of being more in charge of your own thoughts and actions, even when strong feelings rise up and your tendency is to switch to an autopilot mode of stress reaction patterns.

Practicing these exercises develops various capacities that include control of your thoughts, control of your actions, equanimity, open-mindedness and being able to learn from your challenges.

You can learn more about the Six Basic Exercises in *Start Now: A Book of Soul and Spiritual Exercises* by Rudolf Steiner. Also, in my first book, *Connecting with Young Children: Educating the Will* on pages 147-150 you will find a description of these exercises.

A Practice for Developing Strength, Calm and Inner Peace

Embody the feeling of strength the following words from Rudolf Steiner express (from *Verses and Meditations,* Rudolf Steiner). Let that strength literally pour into you, filling your heart and then ray out into all parts of you. Practice this daily and try to really feel the strength and quiet in the depths of your body.

Quiet I bear within me.
I bear within myself
Forces to make me strong.
Now will I be imbued
with their glowing warmth.
Now will I fill myself
With my own will's resolve.
And I will feel the quiet
Pouring through all my being,
When by my steadfast striving,
I become strong
To find within myself
The source of strength,
The strength of inner quiet.

Take a quiet few minutes for yourself a couple of times a day. Use the bathroom as a place of quiet and privacy if you need to. Do this either with your eyes open or shut. When you have your quiet space, fill it with thinking about peace and inner strength. Read or speak the above words while embodying feelings of **peace and strength**. What are those qualities for you? What do they feel like? Embody those feelings of strength and peace, let them wash over and through your physical body. Let the feelings pour into you, filling your heart and then raying out into all parts of you. What does that feel like? Feel how those feelings live in your physical body. Practice this daily - remember to really feel it in your body. A regular embodying of positive feeling can change your neurology to be able to be more present, calm and strong - even when the going gets tough.

H.E.A.L.

Why does the practice of 'embodying strength, calm and peace' create changes in you? According to Rick Hanson, the neuropsychology of learning works in this way:

1. **H**ave a positive experience. It can be the delicious cup of tea, or it can be thinking about that delicious cup of tea.

2. **E**nrich the experience to build it into the neural structure. Make the feeling last and feel it strongly in your imagination. Try to involve various senses in recreating the experience.

3. **A**bsorb and enjoy the experience, and the reflecting about the experience. Keep kindling the feeling and warm yourself with the feelings.

4. **L**ink this positive experience with the negative qualities you want to neutralize. Think about what it means for you.

Work With the Environment

The possibilities of the awake, mindful adult, due to the presence of a mature prefrontal cortex, are thinking ahead *and* really responding to the needs of the moment. As I mentioned earlier, we can create and **modify the environment** for the children to make it safer and eliminate some conflict areas. Perhaps you keep your special Revere Ware pans that your grandmother gave you in a low cupboard.

When your baby starts crawling, and opening everything in reach you have 2 options. Saying 'No' whenever she starts to open that cupboard (which she will do a lot). Or, moving the pans so they are out of reach.

When you notice your child often doesn't finish the food you serve him, start serving him less. Then when he finishes and is still hungry, you can serve a bit more.

You Can't Fix Someone Else's Feelings

Another practice is learning to allow those to whom you relate to have their feelings without you needing to 'fix it' for them. Accept and acknowledge their feelings, and in your response keep their feelings separate from their actions. When your child is melting down, or whining for something, or having a tantrum, simply acknowledge what they are feeling. "You really wanted ice cream." "You wanted to go with Mommy." If you affirm what they are feeling, they will feel heard and that is a deep magic. Try it and see. It is the same with adults. If someone listens to us and reflects back to us what we are feeling, we feel heard. They don't have to agree with our wants or ideas, but being heard is a powerful magic for everyone.

For more on this, read Janet Lansbury's wonderful article: http://www.janetlansbury.com/2014/06/a-mental-health-mantra-for-parents-and-kids/

Observe and You WILL Learn

The development of the capacity for active observing the child goes a long way toward being able to know what the child really needs. It is not easy to observe without judging and finding fault and diagnosing. The more we learn to see what really is in front of us rather than what we are thinking about what we see, then we can begin to truly know someone *in the moment*. Not who we already decided they are, but who is in front of us *right now*, and who they are becoming. Disabling our tendency to judge and prejudge is part of the mindfulness of real awareness.

Is the child hungry? Tired? Getting sick? Paying attention can lead to modifying your daily rhythm, and thereby averting meltdowns and other challenging catastrophes, as well as avoiding you falling into your reaction patterns.

A Key to Unlock Barriers to Connection

Non Violent Communication is a practice that has at its foundation finding the connection first, and the solutions later. NVC, sometimes called Compassionate Communication, is much more than a communication technique, it is a practice to reframe your thinking and your perspective on situations and is a path to move beyond blame and shame habits to an art of real connecting.

The basic premise is that we try to become conscious of our own feelings and needs and how those drive our actions and reaction patterns. Marshall Rosenberg, who articulated NVC, offered the idea that all action is driven by attempts to get one's needs met. When we change how we think and are able to see behavior as strategy to get needs met, then we stop our blaming and fault-finding. We can apply this to everyone we interact with or think about.

NVC has the primary goal of creating and enhancing connection. One of our most basic human needs is connection yet so often how we think and what we say creates obstacles to that connecting.

In examining our experiences, we can be clear about what we observe, what feelings arise from those observations, what needs or values drive those feelings, and then try to do something about all that by making specific requests of others. Mostly though, people criticize, judge, offer opinions, make assumptions give diagnoses, blame, shame and make demands. No one likes to be shamed or have demands put on them!

Marshall laid out a structure for speaking the 'hard' things in ways that support connection, and he aptly described how the communication patterns that do not enhance connecting are so prevalent and tenacious in our world whether on a personal level, or in large group interactions.

NVC classes and workshops are offered worldwide. Find out what is offered in your area.

Connecting with our own feelings and needs is the key to the path of knowing thyself.The more connected with our own feelings and needs we can be, the greater the potential for connecting, true connecting, with others.

Warm-Hearted Thinking

Here is another practice in which we live into our own heart center. From a warmth point of view, our head is cold, thinking is cold, and the feelings, the heart, is the center of warmth. We can learn to warm up our thinking in the following way.

First, we prepare by creating compassion for that child who is challenging for us. Perhaps we are not able to truly meet his needs. Perhaps he very effectively can 'push our buttons.' He is not physically present during this practice, we are actively picturing this child in our imagination. We call up from inside of our self a warm wish for him not to suffer. Feel caring feelings flow from the center of your heart toward him.

A great time of day to do this is just before sleep. Take these warm feelings you have called up towards the child into your sleep. Sleep on it. Who knows what can happen in your sleep...

We All Have Habits

According to one study, 40% of our daily actions are habits. 40% of the things we do every day are done habitually, without conscious awareness and thought. That is a lot of time spent in **autopilot** mode. There are some benefits to this. When we are acting from habit, part of our consciousness is freed up for thinking, planning, reviewing and so on. Do you notice how much thinking you do in the shower? It is because nearly all of your shower activity is habit. You don't have to think about it and therefore your mind is free to wander.

Many habits are created as a strategy to meet a goal. Once the strategy proves successful we repeat and repeat until we just do it without thinking. That is a habit. We are not born with our habits, we develop them in response to experiences. Usually habit forming is not intentional - there is no conscious choice made to form the habit.

Imitation is the central learning tool of young child. Through imitation the young child learns walking, speaking, and stress response patterns and so much more. All habits.

With very young children, many of their habits are created by imitating those around them. Habits are also created by babies attempting to get their needs met and discovering certain strategies that are successful with the adults in the baby's environment. They try it. It works. They repeat and repeat and repeat. So by the time we are adults, we have many habits including ones for dealing with stress, challenges and not getting our needs met. Often these strategies are not helpful and are unproductive for social harmony and true problem solving.

When you get stressed do you 'check out' and fall into your habit reaction pattern? You can be honest here. No one can hear you. We all do it. What is your particular, unique stress reaction? Do you yell and stomp around? Throw things? Tell someone else it is their fault? Freeze up? Withdraw? Fall silent and walk away? When we start to see those habits, those behavior patterns, then we have a chance to change them. Habits in themselves aren't always a problem. There are habits that need changing though - the unproductive, ineffective and unhealthy habits.

First step - see your habit patterns, your reaction style. The next step is to use your free decision-making capacity to choose the habits you want to change. It takes the power of will to start the new habit started, but once the new habit is really running strong we can 'fall asleep' and let the new habit run itself.

Now why am I thinking about habits so much? Because the habits of adults strongly affect the children around them! Now here is a weird thing about our brains. We have a certain kind of brain cell called mirror neurons. Mirror neurons 'fire' both when we act and when we observe an action performed by someone else. In older children and adults, mirror neurons help in understanding the actions of other people. For young children mirror neurons function in the learning of new skills by imitation. Our habits are being transmitted by our example to our children who are imitating them. So it is incumbent on us to try and deliver habits to our children that we want them to have.

I want young ones to develop the habit of washing hands before eating, so I model that activity for the children. I want young children to develop habits of saying 'please' and 'thank you,' so I use those phrases myself whenever appropriate. I don't want my daughters to take up my habits of dealing with stress by withdrawing, so I try and model engagement and conversation when I am in a stressful situation.

When breaking and forming habits, we need to know that change is possible. Repeat after me; CHANGE IS POSSIBLE. Change....is.....possible!

The basic mechanism for learning and development is the will. What is the will but our capacity for doing, for taking hold of the world around us through activity. All education is education of the will, both in the adult and in the child. In the adult there is much more possibility for intention to be part of the equation. The primary way the will functions in the young child is through unconscious imitation - the learning modality for the young child is imitation. What we do, what we say, and who we are, as adults standing before them, is of utmost importance. The goal is the development of our adult capacity for freedom, the capacity to respond rather than react. When we present the example of changing ourselves, that possibility is implanted deep in the child's neurology and psyche as a future possibility for themselves.

To enhance connecting with those around you and to create a more harmonious life for yourself, I offer the following **Short List of Big Things to Try and Live Without**:

> Blaming yourself or someone else
>
> Finding fault and diagnosing wrongness
>
> Judgmental thinking
>
> Demands, Threats, Ultimatums
>
> Shoulds and Shouldn'ts
>
> Retribution and Punishment

Help!

When you are feeling challenged by a particular child, your buttons are easily pressed and your reactions take over, here is a practice of asking for help. Before you go to sleep (a great time to do this sort of work) picture the child (or anyone) who is so challenging for you. Picture his smiling face, or hear his speaking voice. Try and hold a true observation of him in your imagination. And then ask him inwardly, in your active imaginative thinking, "What can I do to serve your needs?"

Create an expectant silence, an active silence for answers to be spoken into. Ask and wait and listen - and see if answers come. Try and pay attention for an answer, it might not come in a way you think. Perhaps someone not aware of your challenge will suggest you read a particular book. Perhaps another child will ask to play a certain game. Perhaps you'll receive an email from an old friend with just the right idea. You never know where the help might come from so you have to be open and listening for the help that will be offered. Each evening keep asking, and each day be actively, expectantly open for answers to come.

Reach out for help. Don't forget you have friends and colleagues also. They can be your support network where your challenges can be voiced and you might receive useful suggestions.

Know Yourself

The ancient Greeks wrote over the door to the Temple in Delphi, a temple dedicated to the ancient mysteries, *Know Thyself*. That is the task and it is no easy task, yet to be worthy of the imitation of the young children we have to again and again walk through the door of that temple. Find out who you are and what you are made of. Life will give you plenty of opportunities for self discovery. It is in the challenges, the difficult situations, that we can truly meet ourselves and thereby are given opportunities to develop new capacities in ourselves.

To me, this is true spiritual self education. It means I recognize that there is a part of me that learns, not the math and language skills, etc, but the lessons of life. That we can develop ourselves is the basis - that is human potential.

What is the spirit in me? The spirit in me is that aspect of myself that does the developing, that learns from the challenges, that attempts to see what needs changing and then has the will to change it. The spirit in me is trying to help me become truly human.

We all have shortcomings, yes, but we all have a great gift to share with the world. The world is waiting for these gifts. The children and everyone around us benefit when we try to develop our self and become more present and awake.

Chapter 8

Conflict Resolving

*What happens when things don't
go the way you want them to?*

Put into words what is real for you. **What is it specifically you
don't like in what you experienced?**

Once again I want to mention that the main learning paradigm
for the young child is imitation. This means that how the adults
around them manage conflict is particularly influential in the
child's developing communication skills and ability to resolve
conflicts in effective ways. If the adults are an example of
revealing what is alive for them in their hearts, then that is what
the children will imitate. Because the young children are so
imitative it is so important for them to experience their adults
working on their reaction patterns on response to stress. This is
how the children are guided toward being able to resolve their
own conflicts.

Here is an example from life: Five-year-old Jack was playing
with a wooden boat. Five-year-old Jill approached Jack and
took the boat and went to another part of the room to play. Jack
cried. There are many possible approaches for an adult to take
to help resolve the situation. "Jill! Give that back to Jack and
say you are sorry." Or; "Jill. How do you think Jack feels? What
would you feel like if he did that to you?"

I prefer this approach. To Jill "It is Jack's turn now and you may
have a turn next." Or, to Jill, "Jack is sad. Can you do
something that will help him?"

We cannot expect the young child to be able to understand how
someone else is feeling when she is just beginning to be able
to label her own feelings. Also, to simply require an apology
does not allow Jill to help resolve the situation herself, through

actively engaging in the solution. She doesn't learn anything in being told what to do. Learning involves self-directed activity.

I think it is important not to blame one of the children or to make them "wrong." Instead of, "You hurt him." Or "You should feel ashamed of yourself." What if we try, "He is hurt." "He doesn't like that." Words like "right," "wrong," "good," "bad," appropriate," and "inappropriate" have no place in leading the children toward compassion and self-responsibility. They are value judgments that are merely the opinion of the speaker Through an active developing of compassion for the one hurt, and by giving the children spoken examples of what you would be happy to hear them say, then out of imitation the children can develop communication tools for their communication and conflicts are resolved more easily.

It is a long process to guide the children into habits of communication and conflict resolving and it requires patience, consistency and perseverance from the adults. The qualities can be developed in us and they serve to guide the children into their bright future.

Sticks and Carrots Our parents gave us many of our habits and stress reaction patterns, and we learned from our parents ways to motivate others. How do you get others to do what you want? Do use a stick or a carrot? Do you threaten? Do you bribe? Often we use these methods in subtle ways, and often we use both at various times.

Which is your main tool? We all use both. It is helpful to be aware of your tendency so you have the possibility of changing it if you so choose. Do you want your child to become a threatener or a briber?

To teach young children **conflict resolution,** we have to take advantage of their natural learning method and give them tools we want them to imitate from our example. Rather than explaining and instructing the children, we can show them respectful ways to navigate conflict. We can speak words and phrases we would be happy to hear them imitate.

Try to leave out the vocabulary of right and wrong, good and bad, should and shouldn't, and appropriate and not appropriate.

You might have heard me say this before; *when interacting with a young child, the words right and wrong, good and bad, appropriate and not appropriate, okay and not okay, and should and shouldn't, have no value and no usefulness. Those words do not tell the child anything about what is real for you!.*

All those terms describe opinions about actions, and usually they are opinions that have been adopted from others including our parents, religions, and cultures. They do not help resolve personal challenges and they do not speak of what is true for the individual having the interaction. When having an interaction with someone when things didn't go the way you wanted, all of the above mentioned terms are opinions and do not help to effectively resolve problems and change behaviors.

When things don't go they way you wanted, try letting the other person know what is truly true for you. Did you like or not like what occurred? Let them know that. That reveals to the other something of your inner self, it expresses what is real and true for you. That is being "authentic."

This applies whenever things do not go the way you want and you are trying to communicate that to someone else - **whatever their age** - though when the interaction is adult-to-adult, perhaps you would use a few more words to fill in the picture.

With young children, try to get your point across in a very FEW words - a dozen or less!

And one more piece of advice, when you are letting someone else know what you do not like, focus on the activity you don't like rather than on the person who did the thing you don't like.

They are more likely able to receive what you are saying that way.

Perhaps your three year old walks over when you are talking on the phone and hits you. You, "I don't like hitting." (Probably she is wanting some attention, some connecting.) What a different experience than, "I don't like *you* hitting me." Also different than, "It's not okay to hit," "You shouldn't hit," or, "We don't hit" (someone just did). (Additionally you could offer some words you would like your child to imitate some future time like, "Excuse me Mommy." You could say these words on your child's behalf. You might have to say it over and over in similar situations until eventually they are taken up in imitation by your child.)

Often I have overheard teachers say to a young child, "We don't hit here." That can't be true. I had just seen one child hit another. What is true is, "Teacher does not like hitting," and, "Everybody needs to be safe."

To the child flicking paint all around with her paintbrush, and it is getting on other children's paper, "I don't like when the paint goes onto someone else's paper." Or, on behalf of a child, "Sally doesn't like other people painting on her paper."

"I don't like running inside. I want everyone to be safe. We can run outside."

"The dog doesn't like his tail to be pulled. He wants to be safe."

"I like everyone to sit at the table until we all are done eating."

You likely will have to do the same sort of thing many, many times before it sinks in as a communication habit or strategy for the young children. Changing habits takes time, lots of time, and lots of repetition.

Young children love their parents, and they love their teachers and caregivers. When you tell them what is real for you, what you don't like, that means something for them. They do want to please you even if they have habits you don't like and that are hard to change. If you mention that an action they did is something you don't like, they are more likely to change than if you tell them that it is 'bad,' or 'not okay,' or 'inappropriate.'

When having an interaction with someone when things didn't go the way you wanted, opinions don't help. When you reveal to someone what you don't like, you are revealing who you are, you are exposing your own values.

Try and leave out of your vocabulary words like right and wrong, good and bad, appropriate and not appropriate, okay and not okay, and should and shouldn't.

When you are witnessing a conflict, ask yourself; Do I need to **intervene** in this situation? If we intervene too early and too often, the children can't develop skills for resolving their own conflicts. If we never intervene, then we might be allowing behavior patterns and habits to develop which we'd rather not see such as aggression and violence to get what is wanted, or always giving up the contested object, or, or, or...

So it is an art to determine what situations require intervention, and how to intervene that allows for learning and respects all the individuals involved. Crucial is attentiveness to the situation and the children's needs. I think the primary intention is that everybody needs to be safe, both physically and emotionally. And go from that basis.

Don't forget humor!

Sometimes humor can magically take away the charge and heat of a situation allowing the involved parties to settle down and be with each other in a more peaceful and constructive way. Don't underestimate the power and possibility of humor.

Silliness can go a long way to reduce conflict and help move things forward. So keep a healthy supply of humor up your sleeve for whatever might arise.

Avoid These Techniques

In a world of differing opinions and inevitable conflict, the following are some consistently **unsuccessful strategies**:

1. The Attempt to be Right
2. The Attempt to Control - trying to get someone else to do something different
3. Retaliation
4. Withdrawal and 'Freezing Up'

The basic mechanism for learning is the will - all education is education of the will, both in the adult and in the child. How can we foster situations in which the will of the young child can take hold? How can we foster situations where true learning can arise, even when there is conflict?

How About Leaving Out the Word 'Okay," Okay?

As an experiment, try leaving out the word "*okay*," okay? When we end a sentence with okay it sounds like a question. Often parents make a statement and end it with a rising-in-pitch 'okay.' I don't think an option is really being offered but the way language is used makes it into a question. When we ask a question, we have to be prepared for a 'yes' or a 'no' answer.

"Come on Sally, we have to go, okay?"
How about, "I want you to get out of the pool now. I need to get us home for dinner."

At kindergarten drop-off; "I'm going now, okay?" likely won't turn out the way you want.

Instead try, "I'm going and will be back to get you after storytime."

Whose Needs?

I remember one morning when my youngest daughter was about three years old. She had been playing in the living room. I had an appointment and had to bring her with me, and I like to leave the house tidy when I go, especially common areas like the living room. I looked around at the toys and cloths and clothes and said, "You need to clean up this stuff so we can go."

A flash of realization zapped my head. AHA! *She* did not need to clean up, it was *my* need. I had a need for tidiness and a need to be on time for my appointment. Neither of those were her agenda, needs or values. It was my agenda. Now, I try to own my needs when I speak. "I need to leave soon." "I want the house to be tidy."

Tips for Tidy Away Time

Often there are actions you want your child to take, but he or she is not noticing what is yet undone, or is not participating at all. Coming in from outside, I see a jacket left outside on a bench. I know who it belongs to, and rather than naming the child and telling her to go get it, I say, "There is one jacket left outside." It brings to the child's attention that something is left undone, and the action wanting to happen speaks for itself. And the child who may not have noticed checks for her jacket and discovers it is the one left out. Out of her own motivation, she goes and collects her jacket and hangs it on the hook inside. My words of observation were a stimulus for the child's action.

Perhaps it is tidy-away time, and the child is standing empty-handed, not participating in putting things away, and you want him to help. Again, a spoken observation like, "I see a cloth over there" might help. Sometimes all it takes to bring the child into activity is for their attention to be brought to something that needs to be done, without telling them to do it. Their own inner will takes care of the rest.

I might pick up a log, walk toward the child who is simply standing without helping, and hand him the log. He take hold of it, and I walk on, not having said anything. He is now holding a log, his will engages, and he puts it on the shelf, and then joins in the tidying away. Or several children have made a restaurant at playtime, and you want them to help put things away. They are still at it; taking orders and cooking food. I pick up a plate and spoon and say, "Here is the food Sally wanted at the dishes store." And the child delivers the order to the shelf where the cooking toys are put away. Or, folding up various colored cloths, I say, "I need someone to deliver this cherry pie (the red cloth)." A child presents herself for delivery, and takes the 'pie' to the shelf where it belongs. Other children come to help put them away because I have made a blueberry pie, lime pie, strawberry, and so on. I have entered into the land of imagination where the children live, and for many young children, this can be an instant cure for the 'not-helping-at-tidy-away-time syndrome.'

"Take these boards to the lumber store." "These animals go to the zoo." (The wooden toy animals) You get the idea. It is important also for the adult to be part of the task, rather than assigning it to the children. If the reality is 'we are tidying up' it is far more effective than saying to the child or children, "you tidy this up."

It is far more effective to participate in tidying up *with* your child than to expect or demand that they do it all by themselves. Let's tidy up." and really do it together. Then when the child is a bit older, she will have the habit of putting things away and you can step back from the activity.

What is this counting thing?

Many parents and teachers use the count down (or up) method of attempted behavior control. "One, two, three...." To me there is an implied punishment if what the adult wants the child to do (or stop doing) doesn't happen in time. It is a veiled threat. I am not an advocate of threatening to get the behaviors I want to see. Usually it is an 'idle threat.' There is no 'punishment' awaiting the child's non-compliance, and she knows it, based on previous interactions with her parents. Maybe she likes to hear her dad count. Maybe she is just learning how to count and she enjoys hearing her mom filling in that hard-to-remember number 'two?'

Instead of counting out-loud, try this five minutes before getting-out-of-pool time. Dad and Sally are both in the pool. "Sally, we are going to get out and shower soon. It's almost time for dinner."

Dad and Sally are both still in pool 5 minutes later. "Sally, we're getting out now." Sally cries, "I don't want to get out."
Dad, "I know you don't want to get out. You love the pool. We'll be back again."

Perhaps Dad has to carry Sally out of the pool (they are both still in the pool). She cries and he says, "I know your are sad. I love the pool too. It is time to go home for dinner and we'll be back again." And off to the showers they go.

End of discussion. Sally can cry more if she wants to. Crying is natural when we grieve for what we want and don't get. Dad is caring and he acknowledges Sally's feeling. *And* he is firm and not giving options when there aren't any.

It's not easy to change habits. If we examine our interactions in the clear light of objectivity, it can give the impetus we need to make the changes we want to see in ourselves. We all want connection, especially with our children. So I offer these suggestions to steer clear of potential obstacles and make connecting easier. All of our habitual reaction gets in the way of connection. We simply are not there to connect with. When we can be more mindful and alert to what is going on, we can be present to connecting. And that is what our children truly long for!

Time-Out, Spanking and Punishment

When a young child does something that is other than what the adult wants, there are various possible scenarios. A *punitive* approach is when the adult decides how the offender will be punished. Time-out, spanking and punishment all belong to the punitive approach.

An alternative could be called a *unitive* approach. It helps to know to what happened, ideally with minimal or no questioning and probing of the young children involved because the adult saw it happen and knows who was affected. In a unitive approach, consideration is given to what can be done to make things right again for all parties involved.

Time-out is a popular technique some adults employ for behavior modification. When a time-out is used, usually the adult first demands that the child stop whatever behavior it is that the adult is finding unpleasant. The child is told to stop the misbehaving and be quiet. When the child doesn't stop, he is required to go and sit alone somewhere, away from the adults and other children, and told not to get up until he can better control himself.

What has led to this situation? In most cases it is that the child has become upset and demanding or angry when their needs were not met. All behavior is based on attempting to meet needs. Young children lack the ability to meet their own needs, in trust they depend on adults to make sure their needs are met. Rest, food, warmth, safety in play situations, etc... all are needs that adults must see to for the young child. Additionally, young children tolerate frustration even less well than adults,

*and are less likely to be able to identify their own frustrated
need that is upsetting them.*

*Being put in a time-out prolongs the time that a child feels upset
about their frustrated need that stimulated the 'misbehavior.'
What exacerbates this state of already being frustrated is the
fact that the child is alone, away from the adults who they rely
on for meeting their needs. Separation from the trusted adult, a
main source of comfort and security, adds to the challenge of
the situation for a child. The child feels this as punishment.*

*Moreover, being alone in time-out can lead to feelings of fear
and anxiety. Being alone and in time-out increases the
frustrations felt by a child who is already feeling frustrated. For
the frustrated and uncomfortable child, time-out offers enforced
silence and the need to squash whatever feeling he was having
that led to the time-out. Time-out tells a child that uncomfortable
emotions need to be ignored and denied in himself. Children
learn to ignore their feelings of hurt and anger. They learn to
repress their painful feelings. In some children, nervous habits
arise to distract them form their uncomfortable feelings such as
nail biting and thumb sucking. As a result, being unaware of
feelings can often become a habit for the child as he grows into
adulthood.* (Stephen Spitalny, *Connecting With Young Children:
Educating the Will*, p.131)

As far as spanking, let me be perfectly clear. I recommend that
you **Never Spank Your Child**. Don't spank in anger, and don't
choose to spank while you are calm. Hitting as punishment, a
persuasion method or boundary delivery technique has
unintended side effects. Punishment is not the way. Spanking is
a punishment that means you are making someone suffer for
not doing what you wanted. 'They have done wrong and
therefore must suffer.'

Being a parent is sometimes a struggle. As a grandpa, I am one
step removed from the level of stress parents experience. I am
no longer engaged in the day-to-day activity of parenting while
trying to fulfill the other necessities of daily life. I am guessing

that everyone at one time or another feels like lashing out in anger. I know I sometimes felt that way as a parent. The question is how to deal with that triggered feeling that often leads to a reaction response of hitting - What do you do when that feeling arises?

The primary learning modality for young children is imitation. They copy from the example of the loved ones around them. It is not a conscious choice to copy though. It is if the children are compelled to copy by some invisible impulse. Imitation is an unconscious method of learning for the young child.

The children learn many other things from parents through imitation, including their strategies for dealing with frustration and stress. Simply put, spanking teaches the children that hitting is a way to get the message across when they are frustrated.

Boundaries are important for the children. One of the child's needs is safety and adults have to hold safe boundaries so the children can develop and thrive within those boundaries. There are other ways than spanking or hitting to show the child boundaries. In fact, using hitting as a tool for creating boundaries shows the child that he or she is not safe because if they do certain things they get hit. This creates an anxious world for the child.

Staying calm and centered and responsive is not easy. Stress sends most of us into our reactive mode and if spanking and hitting is programmed into us from our own childhood, then it is very hard to choose non-violent actions. Parenting is truly a spiritual journey because we get the chance to look at our own reactiveness and behavior patterns and work on overcoming those. Parenting is a path of self-development and our children are here to help teach us. If we understand that we are participating in the programming of reaction patterns into our children, maybe that is enough to help us hold back our impulse to spank and punish. Even if we think we are calm and centered and choosing in the moment to apply a spank to get a message across, we are still teaching the child that one hits when others don't do what we want.

Along with any practices you take up to maintain your calm and patience, I also suggest thinking in advance of an alternative you can put in place if the time comes. Plan ahead! There are many resources in print (my book *Connecting With Young Children* for example) and online (Dr. Rick Hanson's website, and the Parenting Beyond Punishment website) to give you ideas for alternative actions and practices for staying in your responsive and centered mode.

Additionally, remember that the part of the brain that does 'executive function,' that is involved in understanding consequences, cause and effect, and logic, is simply not present in the young child. That part of the brain is the last part of the brain to mature and even during adolescence it is still undergoing extensive changes. It continues developing until one is almost thirty years old. Your young child does not have the neurology to understand why they are being spanked.

You can think of an alternative to spanking or punishing. Our whole world will be a better place for it.

What Is Your Intention?

In Marshall Rosenberg's *Nonviolent Communication: A Language of Life* (pps. 161-164), he offers an important distinction between punishment and what he calls the 'protective use of force.'

The intention behind the protective use of force is to prevent injury or injustice. The intention behind the punitive use of force is to cause individuals to suffer for their perceived misdeeds. When we grab a child who is running into the street to prevent the child from being injured, we are applying protective force. The punitive use of force, on the other hand, might involve physical or psychological attack, such as spanking the child or reproofs like, "How could you be so stupid! You should be ashamed of yourself!"

When we exercise the protective use of force, we are focusing on the life or rights we want to protect without passing judgment on either the person or the behavior. We are not blaming or condemning the child rushing into the street; our thinking is solely directed toward protecting the child from danger...
When we submit to doing something solely for the purpose of avoiding punishment, our attention is distracted from the value of the action itself. Instead, we are focusing upon the consequences of what might happen if we fail to take that action. If a worker's performance is prompted by fear of punishment, the job gets done, but morale suffers; sooner or later, productivity will decrease. Self-esteem is also diminished when punitive force is used. If children brush their teeth because they fear shame and ridicule, their oral health may improve but their self-respect will develop cavities.
Furthermore, as we all know, punishment is costly in terms of goodwill. The more we are seen as agents of punishment, the harder it is for others to respond compassionately to our needs.

Boundaries Again

One cold winter morning, 2 year old Jill was wearing her frilly tutu and playing in the kitchen. 5 year-old Jack was getting ready to go with me to the park. Jill said she wanted to go too. Auntie said, "Take off your tutu so you can get your coat on." Jill said she wanted to wear the tutu. Jill can be very stubborn and sometimes screams and yells (very loudly) as an often successful strategy to get what she wants.

Her grandma was in the kitchen and I could sense her lack of certainty as she said, "Let's take off the tutu and put on the coat. Okay, Jill?" I could tell that she was tentative and was ready to let Jill keep the tutu on. (Grandma later confirmed that she was going to let Jill decide whether or not to take off the tutu and wear the coat.)

Auntie began explaining to 2-year-old Jill why she should take off the tutu ("It might get dirty, it would get in the way of playing at the playground, it might get ripped, your coat won't fit well with the tutu under it...") and wear the coat ("It is cold, it is winter, you'll be cold..."). Auntie was trying to convince Jill why it was a good idea to take off the tutu and wear the coat.

Jill said several times, "No," she would not take off the tutu, as both Auntie and Grandma continued to talk to her and moved closer and closer to her. I was watching this dynamic interaction of the three and saw Jill shaking her head, her unwillingness so visible in her face. I was inwardly clear that if she was joining us outside, the tutu was coming off. So I said, "Jack and Steve are going. Anyone who is coming has to take off their tutu and put on a coat." Without hesitation, Jill took off the tutu and I helped her get her coat on. And off we went. Two happy children and me, ready to walk to the park.

So what happened? Jill responded calmly and easily when she heard the firm boundary that to go to the park means no tutu and yes a coat. No negotiating or wiggle room. So she relaxed and went along.

The words I spoke did not create a Steve vs. Jill situation in my choice of words. I didn't say, "Jill, **you** have to take off your tutu to come with us." I said, "Anyone who is coming..." It was not 'me' vs. 'you' for Jill. My words made the situation more objective, and less personal.

Also, explaining and trying to convince a 2-year-old is not effective for various reasons. One reason is the desire of the child takes up the whole thought and feeling world for them. Persuasion does not have a place at their table. As I mentioned earlier, the child's neurology is not sufficiently developed to process logic and reasoning. The frontal lobe is not functional yet. The adult's intellectual approach of explanation does not meet in the child a neural structure suitable for processing the information.

When we are not clear in knowing what is best for the child i the moment, when we lack inner confidence, the child senses this. And this creates insecurity for the child. They need our calm and confident guidance and leadership. Of course we don't know everything and are constantly learning. And hopefully we are observing the results of our choices and decisions as far as how the child is affected. This informs our future choices and decisions for the child. But it important to remember who is the adult. As an adult there are more neurological structures in place, more neural pathways, and many years of more experiences to draw from.

Somewhere there is a middle ground between authoritarian parenting and a parenting style where the child is in charge. This is where the magic lives. This middle path Margret Meyerkort calls 'loving firmness.' Young children need our calm and clear and non-intellectual guidance that takes into account their stage of development, and their needs for safety and fun.

Tell a Story - the Transformative Power of story!

Stories can be powerful tools for teaching and behavior transformation. When there is a behavior in your young child that you would like to see changed, an effective tool can be a story that portrays a similar challenge with an outcome you'd like to see. With young children, it is an effective way to help change behaviors and create new habits without a lot of intellectualizing and explaining. Stories are also a wonderful vehicle to convey the values of the storyteller to the listener, the receiver of the story. A story may not be an immediate and magical change to the unwanted behavior, but is is real magic just the same. As with any approach with the young child, it takes time and repetition for change to come.

Chapter 9

Smile and Enjoy

Being with young children is fun and wonderful and full of rewards. The awe and wonder that young children have for the world around them can be an inspiration for adults, and help to keep your soul young. The children radiate joy and engagement with the world - we owe it to them to enjoy the world too. Smile.

When we make facial expressions, we're transmitting information that can be received by others. For the children's sake, let's pass on the non-verbal information that this is a good place to be - by smiling. While scientists still argue over the number of muscles it takes to smile or frown, it can't be argued that smiling just plain feels better than frowning. If you are feeling down and you force yourself to smile, it sometimes is all you need to lighten up your mood.

Pleasure and delight are the forces that most properly enliven and call forth the organs' physical forms.........The joy of children in and with their environment, must therefore be counted among the forces that build and shape the physical organs. They need teachers [and parents] *that look and act with happiness and, most of all, with honest, unaffected love. Such a love that streams, as it were, with warmth through the physical environment of the children may be said to literally "hatch" the forms of the physical organs.* (Rudolf Steiner, *The Education of the Child,* pps.21/22)

Our world is filled with opportunities to be anxious and fearful. Advertisers and politicians continually tell us what we should be afraid of. Insurance companies, pharmaceutical companies and doctors heap on the anxiety. It can be hard not to be anxious yet it is important to overcome our adult fears and anxieties for the sake of the children, as best we can.

Fear and anxiety are cold feelings. They cause sympathetic nervous system responses in connection with our ancient 'reptile brain.' Fear causes the blood to gather in the heart, leaving the limbs colder due to the decrease in blood supply. The body is ready for fight or flight - the heart asks, 'where do I need to send the blood to most effectively be ready to fight or to flee?'

The soul coldness of fear and anxiety prevents connection - connection requires warmth. The children need connection. They need our genuine interest and caring. They need our warmth, the warmth of our relationship with them.

The children also need a feeling of safety so they can play and develop. No safety, no exploration. No safety, no play (which is the young child's way to discover the science of the physical and social worlds). We have to help the young child experience the world as good and safe. To do that, we adults have to learn to live joyfully as an example for the children.

Part of the problem is that we tend to see what is wrong, threats, negativity and get stuck in it. We are programmed to look for threats and what is wrong. Then we think and speak our negativity, our complaining and our problems. We don't have to though.

We can reprogram ourselves to be joyful. *We can hardwire our own happiness*, as Rick Hanson says. It isn't easy. It is possible. It is part of the path of becoming human. It's worth a try. Do it for yourselves...and do it for the children. The future depends on us!

Live joyfully on the earth.

Chapter 10

RSVP

Do you know who the "best parenting advice" comes from? It comes from You. You are your best expert.

With so many conflicting suggestions coming from peers, family, so-called-experts, physicians, "Facebook," and of course, me; your voice - your true inner knowing - can get lost in all the noise.

The truth is, that YOU are the expert on your relationship with your child. Only you can decide what is best for your child right now, and which path your growth as a family will take.

To confidently parent without negotiation and constant explanations, without blaming and shaming, without being reactive, you must first ask yourself: How **mindful, aware**, and **responsible** for my own feelings and actions am I becoming?

The BEST parenting advice always comes from *within*. When we overcome little by little our programmed reaction patterns, and when we are able to truly see the young child as a unique human being standing before us, then we have the possibility of being a *responder*. Then we have become responsible, or **response**-able. It isn't what happens to us that matters as much as **how we respond** to what happens.

R.S.V.P. Respondez vous s'il vous plait.

Please, be a responder.

Bibliography

Brown, Brene; *Daring Greatly*

Hanson, Rick; *Hardwiring Happiness*

Richo, David; *How to Be an Adult: A Handbook for Psychological and Spiritual Integration*

Rosenberg, Marshall; *Nonviolent Communication; A Language of Life*

Schaenen, Inda; *The 7 0'Clock Bedtime*

Spitalny, Stephen; *Connecting with Young Children: Educating the Will*

Spitalny, Stephen; *What's the Story? Storytelling with Young Children as a Path Toward Living Happily Ever After*

Steiner, Rudolf; *Start Now: A Book of Soul and Spiritual Exercises*

Steiner, Rudolf; *The Education of the Child*

On the Web

chamakanda.com - *my website*

chamakanda.blogspot.com - *my blog*

parentingbeyondpunishment.com

janetlansbury.com

rickhanson.net

davericho.com